THE
BALANCED
LIFE METHOD

WORKBOOK

LORI NOLAN

THE
BALANCED
LIFE METHOD

THE 7-PILLAR BLUEPRINT TO LASTING HEALTH AND WELLNESS

WORKBOOK

FO
UR

CONTENTS

LORI NOLAN

THE
BALANCED
LIFE METHOD

THE 7-PILLAR BLUEPRINT TO LASTING HEALTH AND WELLNESS

INTRODUCTION

COINCIDENCE IS NOT IN GOD'S
VOCABULARY, AND THAT, MY
FRIENDS, IS NO COINCIDENCE.

READING TIME

As you read the Introduction in *The Balanced Life Method,* review, reflect on, and respond to the text by answering the following questions.

REVIEW, REFLECT, AND RESPOND

How does a "well-built house" as a metaphor for a balanced life resonate with you? What areas of your life seem structurally unstable or out of balance?

_____
_____
_____
_____
_____

How did you understand and define health before reading the book?

_____
_____
_____
_____
_____

Evaluate the condition of your "house." How well does it stand against the elements of life (stress, poor physical health, poor mental health, etc.)? What do you attribute your answer to?

_____
_____
_____
_____
_____
_____

> "Whoever comes to Me, and hears My sayings and does them, I will show you whom he is like: He is like a man building a house, who dug deep and laid the foundation on the rock. And when the flood arose, the stream beat vehemently against that house, and could not shake it, for it was founded on the rock."
>
> —Luke 6:47-48 (NKJV)

Consider the scripture above and answer the following questions:

In your own words, what do you think Jesus is trying to say in this scripture?

_____

_____

_____

_____

_____

_____

_____

How well does your life align with Jesus's promise of an unshakeable life built on the Rock? Why?

_____

_____

_____

_____

_____

_____

_____

How do you presently respond to the challenges of life's "floods"? How has Jesus helped you to withstand and overcome these challenges?

_____

_____

_____

_____

_____

_____

_____

What aspects of your health and wellness have discouraged or frustrated you? What patterns have you observed that hinder your ability to make long-lasting changes to your overall health and wellness?

_____

_____

_____

_____

_____

_____

How does the inundation of information on health and wellness topics play a role in taking ownership of your health?

_____

_____

_____

_____

_____

_____

Have you ever considered hidden traumas or unaddressed stressors as a culprit to your health challenges and imbalances? What kind of work have you done to explore those factors?

_____

_____

_____

_____

_____

_____

_____

_____

_____

The author states that "our genes don't dictate our destiny." Did that surprise you? Why or what not?

_____

_____

_____

_____

_____

_____

_____

_____

_____

Name three things that you learned or inspired you in the introduction of this book. What do you intend to do with those revelations?

_____

_____

_____

_____

_____

_____

_____

_____

_____

_____

PILLAR 1

SPIRIT

> IT'S ONLY THROUGH JESUS THAT
> OUR HOUSE OF HEALTH AND
> WELLNESS CAN BE BUILT.

READING TIME

As you read Chapter 1: "Spirit" in *The Balanced Life Method*, review, reflect on, and respond to the text by answering the following questions.

REVIEW, REFLECT, AND RESPOND

What do you think it is about a strong spiritual foundation that catalyzes health and wellness benefits in other areas of life?

_____
_____
_____
_____
_____
_____
_____
_____
_____

Reflect on the statement, "We are a spirit that has a body and soul." How does that complement or contrast with your understanding of who we are as it pertains to body, soul, and spirit? How does it challenge your beliefs?

_____
_____
_____
_____
_____
_____
_____
_____

What parts of your health do you tend to focus on? What practices do you implement, and are they effective? Where are you falling short in your goals?

_____

_____

_____

_____

_____

_____

_____

> *"For physical training is of some value, but godliness has value for all things, holding promise for the present life and the life to come."*
>
> **—1 Timothy 4:8 (NIV)**

Consider the scripture above and answer the following questions:

What does this scripture suggest about the sustainability of physical health in the absence of spiritual health?

_____

_____

_____

_____

_____

_____

_____

What areas of your life have prospered from your investment in and care for your spirit? In what areas are you suffering, and how could you incorporate godliness into those areas?

_____

_____

_____

_____

_____

_____

_____

_____

_____

_____

How do you currently prioritize your spirit in your daily life? Describe the ways you tend and nurture your spirit.

_____

_____

_____

_____

_____

_____

_____

_____

_____

_____

_____

Have you experienced the consequences of neglecting your spiritual health? What are they?

_____

_____

_____

_____

_____

_____

_____

_____

What role does Jesus play in your wellness journey? Have you surrendered your journey to Him? If so, what changes have you noticed? If not, what is holding you back from asking for His help?

_____

_____

_____

_____

_____

_____

_____

_____

What does it mean for followers of Jesus to exercise their authority over all things that are not from Him?

_____

_____

_____

_____

_____

_____

_____

_____

Envision victory over everything holding you back from a balanced life. Describe what you see.

_____

_____

_____

_____

_____

_____

_____

_____

The author identifies three key factors that impact our spirit health (thoughts, words, and toxic emotions). Complete the following exercises and answer the questions based on these factors: thoughts, words, toxic emotions.

THOUGHTS

What destructive thoughts do you rehearse about yourself? List three that have repeatedly emerged and write God's counterargument (either from Scripture or from the general perspective of God's love for you).

_____

_____

_____

_____

_____

_____

_____

_____

Consider Philippians 4:8. Write down things in your life that are true, honorable, just, pure, lovely, commendable, and worthy of praise. Then, ask God to show you how those qualities can and will show up in your health journey.

_____

_____

_____

_____

_____

_____

_____

_____

_____

_____

WORDS

Write down three to five areas of your life that are suffering or places where you feel stuck. What words are you speaking about those areas? Write those down and replace them with new statements. Commit to capturing your destructive words and quickly replacing them with constructive and loving words.

_____

_____

_____

_____

_____

_____

_____

_____

What can you learn from the author's clients who tended to their spirits? What can you learn from those who didn't? Which did you most identify with and why?

_____

_____

_____

_____

_____

_____

_____

TOXIC EMOTIONS

Can you identify some toxic emotions that you have yet to address and heal from? The author mentions bitterness, resentment, anger, and unforgiveness. Do any of these resonate with you? If so, explain.

_____

_____

_____

_____

_____

_____

_____

What steps have you taken toward healing those wounds that have allowed toxic emotions to fester and prosper? What may be holding you back from exploring these emotions more deeply?

_____

_____

_____

_____

_____

_____

_____

_____

What role do you think darkness (Satan) might be playing in failed attempts to find and sustain a balanced life?

_____

_____

_____

_____

_____

_____

_____

_____

_____

_____

PILLAR 2

NUTRITION

**REMEMBER, IF GOD MADE IT, YOU'RE GOOD!
IF A FACTORY MADE IT, USE CAUTION.**

READING TIME

As you read Chapter 2: "Nutrition" in *The Balanced Life Method,* review, reflect on, and respond to the text by answering the following questions.

REVIEW, REFLECT, AND RESPOND

How does knowing that your behaviors and choices can shape and control your genes give you hope for your health? How does it challenge your beliefs about genetic contributors to health?

_____

_____

_____

_____

_____

_____

_____

_____

_____

What is your experience with diets and health fads? What did you learn about your body? What did you learn that you *didn't* know about your body?

_____

_____

_____

_____

_____

_____

_____

_____

_____

How would you describe your relationship with food? Where do you think that comes from?

_____

_____

_____

_____

_____

_____

_____

_____

_____

> *"Or do you not know that your body is a temple of the Holy Spirit within you, whom you have from God? You are not your own, for you were bought with a price. So glorify God in your body."*
>
> **—1 Corinthians 6:19-20 (ESV)**

Consider the scripture above and answer the following questions:

What does it look like to use food to glorify God in our bodies?

_____

_____

_____

_____

_____

_____

What is the connection between ownership over our bodies and the food we consume? Why should we care about who owns our bodies?

_____

_____

_____

_____

_____

_____

_____

_____

_____

_____

On a scale of 1 (not well at all) to 10 (extremely well), how well do you think you glorify God in your body? Explain your answer. What would need to change in order to better glorify His temple?

1   2   3   4   5   6   7   8   9   10

_____

_____

_____

_____

_____

_____

_____

_____

_____

How does your body tend to feel on the average day (not when you are ill)? What symptoms present themselves regularly (sluggishness, headaches, fatigue, etc.)?

_____

_____

_____

_____

_____

_____

How would you rate your nutrition, and why?

_____

_____

_____

_____

_____

_____

What kind of foods do you gravitate towards when you are having a bad day? What proportion of your food is manufactured in a factory? How often do you consume these foods and how do they impact you?

_____

_____

_____

_____

_____

_____

The author discusses the importance of creating a "why" to establish and stick to a discipline. What is your "why" for finding lasting wellness?

_____

_____

_____

_____

_____

_____

_____

_____

_____

_____

Consider the food and drink listed in this chapter (protein, carbohydrates, fats, coffee, and alcohol). Journal your intake of these foods and drinks using the template below:

PROTEIN

Sources: **Daily quantity of each source:**

_____

_____

_____

_____

_____

_____

_____

_____

_____

CARBOHYDRATES

Sources: **Daily quantity of each source:**

_____

_____

_____

_____

_____

_____

_____

_____

_____

_____

FATS

Sources: **Daily quantity of each source:**

_____

_____

_____

_____

_____

_____

_____

_____

_____

_____

_____

COFFEE
Brand/kind:

_____

_____

_____

 # Cups/day: **Time(s) of consumption:**

_____

_____

_____

_____

_____

_____

_____

_____

ALCOHOL
Kind (beer, wine, liquor):   **# Drinks/week:**

_____

_____

_____

_____

_____

_____

_____

_____

Cross-reference and compare your report with the author's analysis of both the healthy and unhealthy forms of consuming each. How do your habits measure up? Where do you see the need for improvement?

_____

_____

_____

_____

_____

_____

_____

_____

_____

_____

What is your experience with intermittent fasting? How long is your window between dinner and breakfast?

_____

_____

_____

_____

_____

_____

_____

_____

_____

_____

Consider keeping a food journal for two weeks and pay attention to how you feel throughout your day (morning, afternoon, and evening). What patterns do you observe?

_____

_____

_____

_____

_____

_____

_____

_____

_____

_____

_____

_____

_____

PILLAR 3

STRESS

IF GOD HIMSELF TELLS US TO HAVE A
JOYFUL HEART, WE SHOULD LISTEN.

READING TIME

As you read
Chapter 3:
"Stress" in *The
Balanced Life
Method*, review,
reflect on, and
respond to the
text by answering
the following
questions.

REVIEW, REFLECT, AND RESPOND

Review the differences between distress and eustress in this chapter. Write down three sources of distress and three sources of eustress. Why did you think each source belongs in the category you placed them in?

_____

_____

_____

_____

_____

What stressors have you wrongly classified as distress? What stressors have you wrongly classified as eustress? Why is it so important to classify stressors correctly?

_____

_____

_____

_____

_____

Review the side effects of stress listed in the chart. Do you or have you experienced any of them, and if so, which ones?

_____

_____

_____

_____

_____

> *"Do not be anxious about anything, but in everything, by prayer and supplication, with thanksgiving let your requests be made known unto God, and the peace of God, which surpasses all understanding, will guard your hearts and minds through Christ Jesus."*
>
> —Philippians 4:6-7 (ESV)

Consider the scripture above and answer the following questions:

According to this scripture, we have nothing to be anxious about. Do you believe this? Why or why not? What does your answer say about your relationship with God?

_____

_____

_____

_____

_____

_____

_____

What do you think it means to have a heart and mind guarded through Christ Jesus? Describe, in detail, a time in your life when you have experienced this kind of peace.

_____

_____

_____

_____

_____

_____

_____

_____

What sources of stress have gone unaddressed in your life?

_____

_____

_____

_____

_____

_____

_____

What kind of strategies do you have in place to manage and decrease your stress levels? Are they working? Why or why not?

_____

_____

_____

_____

_____

_____

_____

Review the brief list of foods that nourish and heal the body (dark leafy greens, chia seeds, avocados, nuts, dark chocolate, green tea, beans). How often do you incorporate these foods into your diet? How can you start?

_____

_____

_____

_____

_____

_____

_____

Refer to the list of scriptures that give life and reduce stress when spoken out loud. Which stands out or touches you in a special way? Why does it jump out at you?

_____

_____

_____

_____

_____

_____

_____

_____

Consider the tips and strategies the author recommends for reducing stress (reading the Bible, resting, keeping a journal, exercising, breathing techniques, boundaries, and making time for fun). In which of these categories do you have good practices in place? Where could you improve and how?

_____

_____

_____

_____

_____

_____

_____

_____

_____

THE
BALANCED
LIFE METHOD

PILLAR 4

SLEEP

> IF YOU KEEP DENYING YOUR BODY PROPER SLEEP, IT WILL EVENTUALLY SHUT DOWN AND MAKE YOU SICK. IT WILL THEN FORCE YOU TO SLEEP AND REST.

READING TIME

As you read Chapter 4: "Sleep" in *The Balanced Life Method*, review, reflect on, and respond to the text by answering the following questions.

REVIEW, REFLECT, AND RESPOND

On a scale of 1 to 5 (1 = not at all well, 5 = extremely well), how would you rate the quality of your sleep, on average? What factors do you think play a role in that score? On average, how many hours of sleep do you get at night?

1   2   3   4   5

_____
_____
_____
_____
_____
_____
_____
_____

What kind of routine do you have in place in preparation for sleep? How consistently do you follow this routine each night?

_____
_____
_____
_____
_____
_____
_____
_____

Consider the scripture above and answer the following questions:

How do you think this scripture relates to sleep?

_____

_____

_____

_____

_____

_____

_____

_____

_____

How closely does your life align with the descriptors in this scripture (well-balanced, self-disciplined, alert, cautious)?

_____

_____

_____

_____

_____

_____

_____

_____

_____

How do you fuel your body when you are suffering from sleep deprivation?

_____

_____

_____

_____

_____

_____

_____

_____

_____

_____

_____

_____

Consider the eleven top contenders for disrupted sleep listed in this chapter and write a checkmark next to the items you regularly practice. Which of these could you commit to changing today?

_____

_____

_____

_____

_____

_____

_____

_____

_____

_____

What did you learn about the impact of watching TV and using your computer or phone before bed? Which of the author's recommendations could you begin to implement?

_____

_____

_____

_____

_____

_____

_____

_____

The author identifies caffeine, alcohol, and food consumption as common culprits of disrupted sleep. Do you partake in any of these habits? Refer to the author's suggested practices and identify one practice per habit you will commit to.

_____

_____

_____

_____

_____

_____

_____

_____

Do you have a spouse or a pet who disrupts your sleep? What adjustments can you make to limit these interruptions?

_____

_____

_____

_____

_____

_____

_____

_____

_____

_____

_____

FITNESS

> JUST LIKE THE OTHER PILLARS, THERE'S NO WAY TO SIDESTEP FITNESS AND ACHIEVE OPTIMAL HEALTH.

READING
TIME

As you read
Chapter 5:
"Fitness" in *The
Balanced Life
Method*, review,
reflect on, and
respond to the
text by answering
the following
questions.

REVIEW, REFLECT, AND RESPOND

What is your general attitude towards fitness?

_____

_____

_____

_____

_____

_____

How satisfied are you with your lifestyle as it pertains to fitness? Where does fitness fit into your daily life?

_____

_____

_____

_____

_____

_____

What kind of physical and mental barriers do you encounter when initiating or maintaining a consistent fitness routine?

_____

_____

_____

_____

_____

_____

> *"The name of the LORD is a strong tower;*
> *The righteous run to it and are safe."*
>
> **—Proverbs 18:10 (NKJV)**

Consider the scripture above and answer the following questions:

What do you think the writer of Proverbs meant when he referred to the LORD as a "strong tower"? What kind of strength do you think he was referencing?

_____

_____

_____

_____

_____

_____

_____

_____

Drawing from this scripture, how do you think Christ's physical strength is related to His emotional and mental strength? What does that say about our responsibility to keep our bodies strong as Christ's ambassadors

_____

_____

_____

_____

_____

_____

_____

_____

What kind of exercises do you enjoy that might be a good fit for your body and lifestyle?

_____

_____

_____

_____

_____

_____

_____

_____

When could you devote thirty minutes each day to a fitness routine? Plug your answers into your planner/calendar.

_____

_____

_____

_____

_____

_____

_____

_____

What are your top three fitness goals, and what new lessons can you pull from this chapter into your fitness routine to achieve those goals?

_____

_____

_____

_____

_____

Of all the listed benefits of exercise, which are most important to you and why?

_____

_____

_____

_____

_____

_____

If you could create a "why" statement for remaining physically active, what would it say? What would drive you the most toward maintaining a routine?

_____

_____

_____

_____

_____

What proportion of time do you spend weight training versus cardio? Which is most intimidating for you and why?

_____

_____

_____

_____

_____

_____

What is one small change you can make today? What kind of accountability system could you put in place to ensure that change becomes a lifelong habit?

_____

_____

_____

_____

_____

How closely do you pay attention to ingredients that disrupt the endocrine system?

_____

_____

_____

_____

_____

How do you tend to respond when you plateau after a period of positive results? Reflecting on the lessons from this chapter, what are some ways you could respond differently?

_____

_____

_____

_____

_____

PILLAR 6

RELATIONSHIPS

> WE LOVE FROM OUR HEARTS.
> LOVE IS NOT JUST A FEELING; IT IS
> AN ACTION AND A CHOICE.

READING TIME

As you read Chapter 6: "Relationships" in *The Balanced Life Method*, review, reflect on, and respond to the text by answering the following questions.

REVIEW, REFLECT, AND RESPOND

What does the Genesis story of Adam and Eve tell you about the importance of relationships? Why do you think God insisted that Adam be given a helpmate?

_____

_____

_____

_____

_____

_____

_____

_____

_____

How would you rate the quality of your relationships right now? Which ones make you stronger, and which ones bring you down?

_____

_____

_____

_____

_____

_____

_____

_____

_____

_____

Who has hurt you in the past, and how has it affected your ability to love and be loved?

_____

_____

_____

_____

_____

_____

_____

_____

> *"For if they fall, one will lift up his fellow. But woe to him who is alone when he falls and has not another to lift him up. . . . And though a man might prevail against one who is alone, two will withstand him— a threefold cord is not quickly broken."*
>
> —Ecclesiastes 4:10, 12 (ESV)

Consider the scripture above and answer the following questions:

Think of a time you've fallen. Who was there to pick you up? What did that experience teach you about the safety found in being loved?

_____

_____

_____

_____

_____

_____

_____

Why does the scripture say that it takes two to withstand, but then states that a threefold cord is not quickly broken? Who is the third person?

_____

_____

_____

_____

_____

_____

_____

_____

_____

_____

Who in your life do you find difficult to love as you love yourself? What would it look like to take control of your reactions or, if needed, forgive? How might that free you to love that person and find peace in your heart and mind?

_____

_____

_____

_____

_____

_____

_____

_____

_____

_____

In what relationships in your life do you think the enemy is creating division? How does the source (enemy) of this division change the way you perceive that person or that relationship?

_____

_____

_____

_____

_____

_____

_____

_____

In what ways have you allowed the enemy to "make a grand entrance" into your mind, and how is it impacting your relationships?

_____

_____

_____

_____

_____

_____

_____

_____

_____

Why do you think the enemy's first target of attack is relationships?

_____

_____

_____

_____

_____

_____

_____

_____

_____

_____

Have you ever explored your soul wounds? Take some time to write them down or ask God to reveal them to you.

_____

_____

_____

_____

_____

_____

_____

_____

_____

_____

_____

How is unforgiveness impacting your life? Why do you think God commands unconditional forgiveness? In what ways does it protect you?

_____

_____

_____

_____

_____

_____

_____

_____

In your own words, what is the difference between reconciliation and restoration? Which of your relationships need reconciliation, and which need both reconciliation and restoration?

_____

_____

_____

_____

_____

_____

_____

_____

_____

Who in your life do you need to set a boundary with? Take a few moments to follow the three steps of setting boundaries.

_____

_____

_____

_____

_____

_____

_____

Take inventory of your relationships and answer these two questions: 1) are they making you into who you want to be? and 2) do they bring you distress?

_____

_____

_____

_____

_____

_____

_____

_____

_____

_____

_____

PILLAR 7

PURPOSE

> **PURPOSE ISN'T SO MUCH WHAT YOU'RE GOOD AT; IT'S WHO YOU ARE AND WHO YOU ARE BECOMING.**

READING
TIME

As you read
Chapter 7:
"Purpose" in *The
Balanced Life
Method*, review,
reflect on, and
respond to the
text by answering
the following
questions.

REVIEW, REFLECT, AND RESPOND

How clear are you on your purpose? What is it? If you aren't sure, where are you getting stuck?

_____

_____

_____

_____

_____

What was your initial impression of the DO-BE-HAVE principle of living? In what ways have you lived by this principle? Why do you think it is ineffective?

_____

_____

_____

_____

_____

When people ask you to tell them about yourself, how do you usually respond? What does your response indicate about the way you view your life's purpose?

_____

_____

_____

_____

_____

_____

Consider the scripture above and answer the following questions:

What does this scripture suggest about the limitations of the "DO-BE-HAVE" way of living?

_____

_____

_____

_____

_____

Based on this scripture, how do you think the author would advise you to find your purpose?

_____

_____

_____

_____

_____

What does this scripture imply about the intersection between our purpose and who God is?

_____

_____

_____

_____

_____

_____

Why is it that our purpose can only be found in something outside of ourselves?

_____

_____

_____

_____

_____

_____

If you have not yet completed John Maxwell's core values exercise in this chapter, take some time now to complete it. How well did you know your core values prior to this exercise?

_____

_____

_____

_____

_____

_____

What were your top five values? What steps can you begin to take to become those values?

_____

_____

_____

_____

_____

_____

Write your new purpose statement using the template provided in this chapter. How well does it align with the way you live your life now?

_____

_____

_____

_____

_____

_____

_____

Answer the following questions posed by the author at the end of this chapter:

1. What do you want other people to remember about you and say about you when you are no longer here?

_____

_____

_____

_____

_____

_____

_____

_____

_____

2. What will others *actually* remember and say, based on where you are right now?

_____

_____

_____

_____

_____

_____

_____

_____

_____

_____

3. Is there a discrepancy between what you want them to say and what they would say if you were to remain where you are right now?

_____

_____

_____

_____

_____

_____

_____

_____

_____

_____

Name three small changes you will begin to make to bring you one step closer to a well-balanced life

_____

_____

_____

_____

_____

_____

_____

_____

_____

_____

_____

_____

_____

_____

_____

_____

_____

_____

_____

_____

_____

_____

www.ingramcontent.com/pod-product-compliance
Lightning Source LLC
Chambersburg PA
CBHW070050100426
42734CB00040B/2958